Earthquakes

Julie Haydon

Rigby®

www.Rigby.com
1-800-531-5015

Rigby Focus Forward

This Edition © 2009 Rigby, a Harcourt Education Imprint

Text © 2007 Julie Haydon
Published in 2007 by Nelson Australia Pty Ltd ACN: 058 280 149
A Cengage Learning company

1 2 3 4 5 6 7 8 374 14 13 12 11 10 09 08 07
Printed and bound in China

Earthquakes
ISBN-13   978-1-4190-3822-8
ISBN-10   1-4190-3822-2

Acknowledgments
Illustrations by Boris Silvestri
The author and publisher would like to acknowledge permission to reproduce material from the following sources:
Photographs by Alamy Images/Pacific Press Service/Yoshiaki Nagashima, cover; AP Photo/Steven Wang, p. 14; Alamy Images/Pacific Press Service/Yoshiaki Nagashima, p. 1; Corbis/Bettmann, p. 5, 13/ Shahpari Sohaie, pp. 18-19; Getty Images/John Barr, p. 4 right/ AFP, p. 16/ Majid/Stringer, p. 19/ Majid, p. 20/ AFP/Jean-Francois Camp, p. 21 top/ Majid, p. 21 bottom/ AFP/Martin Bureau, p. 22/ Scott Peterson, p. 23; iStockphoto, p. 3, 12; Photolibrary, pp. 10, 18 top left, Newspix/AFP Photo/Yoshikazu, p. 17.

Earthquakes

Julie Haydon

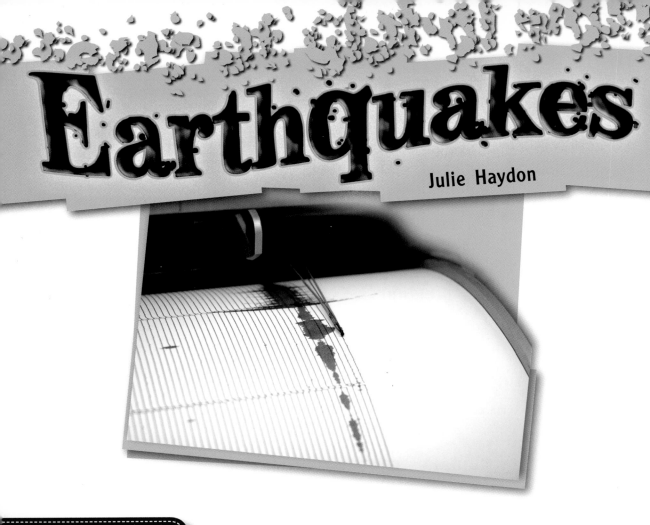

Contents

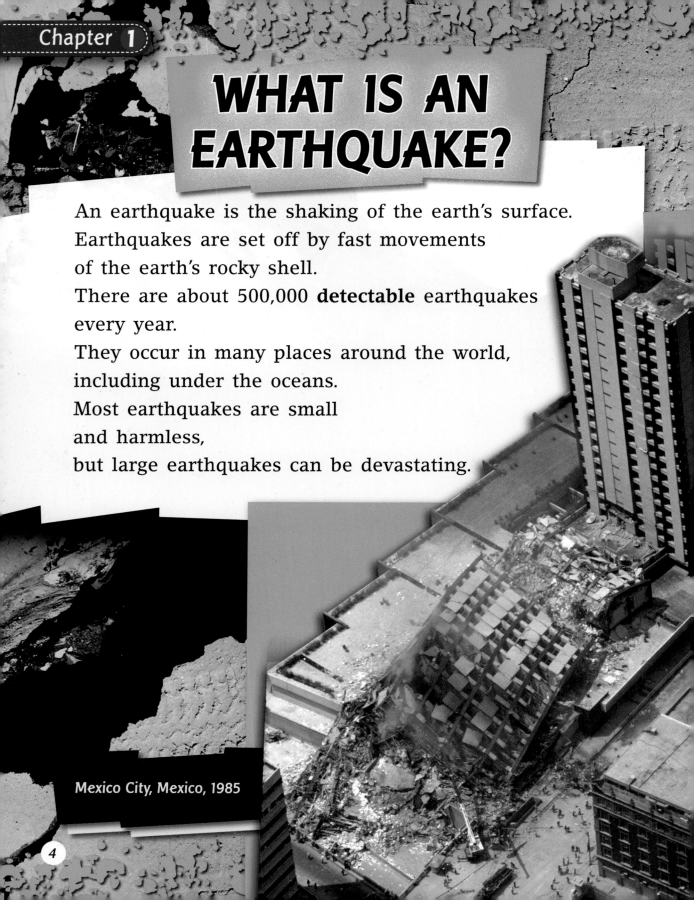

Chapter 1

WHAT IS AN EARTHQUAKE?

An earthquake is the shaking of the earth's surface.
Earthquakes are set off by fast movements
of the earth's rocky shell.
There are about 500,000 **detectable** earthquakes
every year.
They occur in many places around the world,
including under the oceans.
Most earthquakes are small
and harmless,
but large earthquakes can be devastating.

Mexico City, Mexico, 1985

Scientists study the earth's layers
to understand earthquakes.
Recently scientists have been able to explain
how and why earthquakes happen.

Tangshan, China, 1976

The science of earthquakes is called seismology.
Scientists who study earthquakes are called
seismologists.

Chapter 2

THE EARTH'S LAYERS

Long ago, people believed that the earth was solid, but today, scientists know that the earth is made up of layers.

The center of the earth is called the core.
The core is very hot.
The inner core is a solid ball made mostly of iron, and the outer core is made mostly of liquid iron.

The mantle surrounds the core and is made of very hot rock.
The lower part of the mantle is soft and can move very slowly.
The mantle and the core make up most of the earth.

OUTER CORE

INNER CORE

MANTLE

CRUST

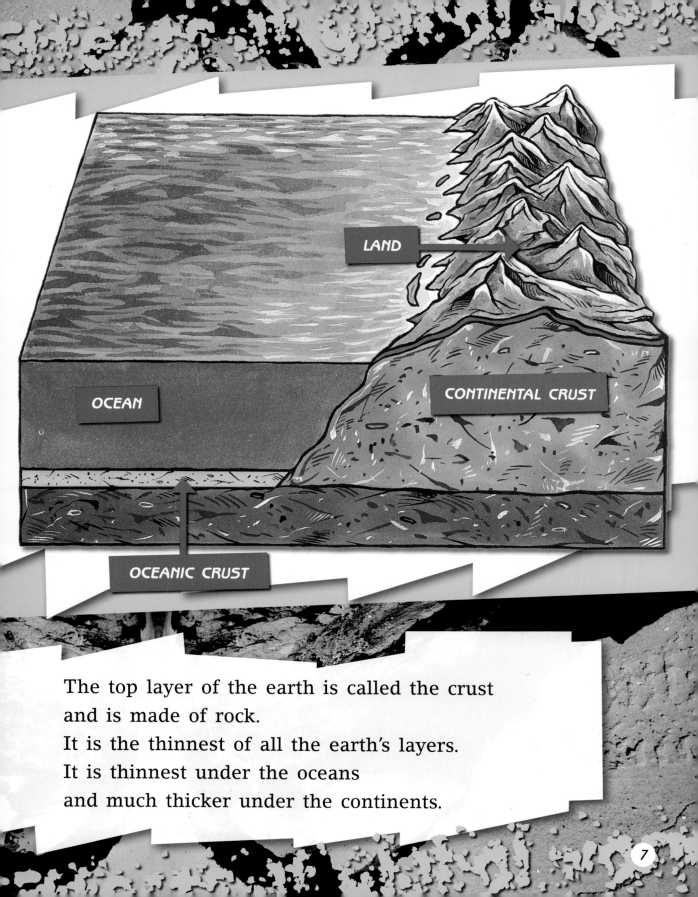

The top layer of the earth is called the crust
and is made of rock.
It is the thinnest of all the earth's layers.
It is thinnest under the oceans
and much thicker under the continents.

Chapter 3

TECTONIC PLATES

The crust and the upper part of the mantle
are made up of huge, plate-like pieces of rock
that float on the lower part of the mantle,
so they are always moving.
Most of the time, the movements of the pieces
are so slow that people cannot feel them.
These huge pieces of rock are called tectonic plates.
They are different sizes, and each one has a name.

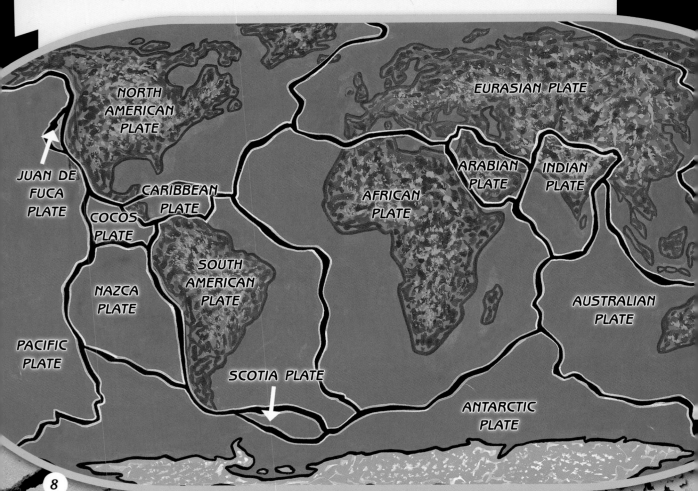

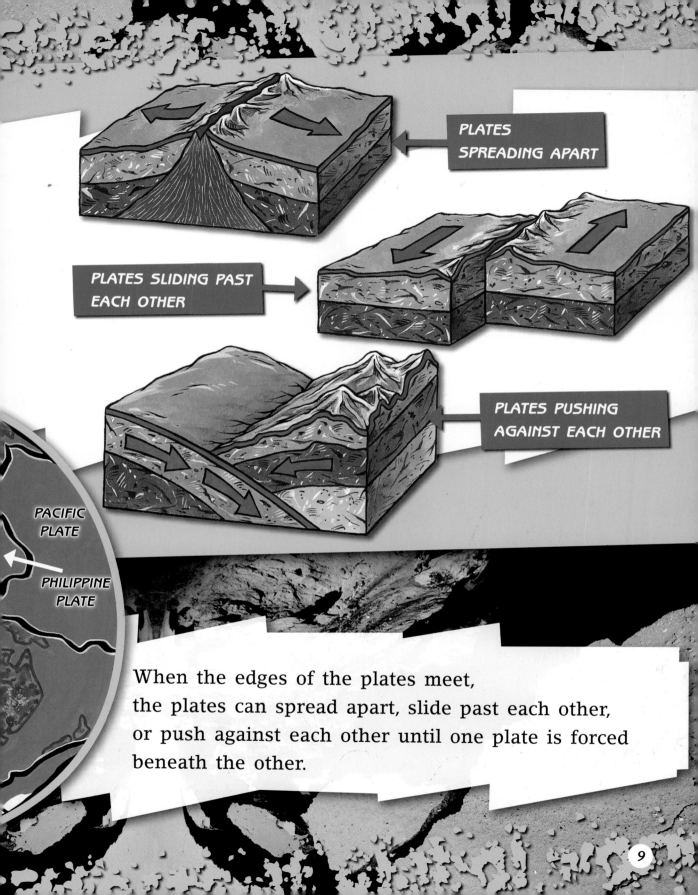

PLATES
SPREADING APART

PLATES SLIDING PAST
EACH OTHER

PLATES PUSHING
AGAINST EACH OTHER

PACIFIC
PLATE

PHILIPPINE
PLATE

When the edges of the plates meet,
the plates can spread apart, slide past each other,
or push against each other until one plate is forced
beneath the other.

Chapter 4

FAULTS

The movements of the tectonic plates make cracks in the earth's rocky crust.
These cracks are called faults,
and they form at the edges of the plates.
Some faults are easy to see.

San Andreas Fault, California

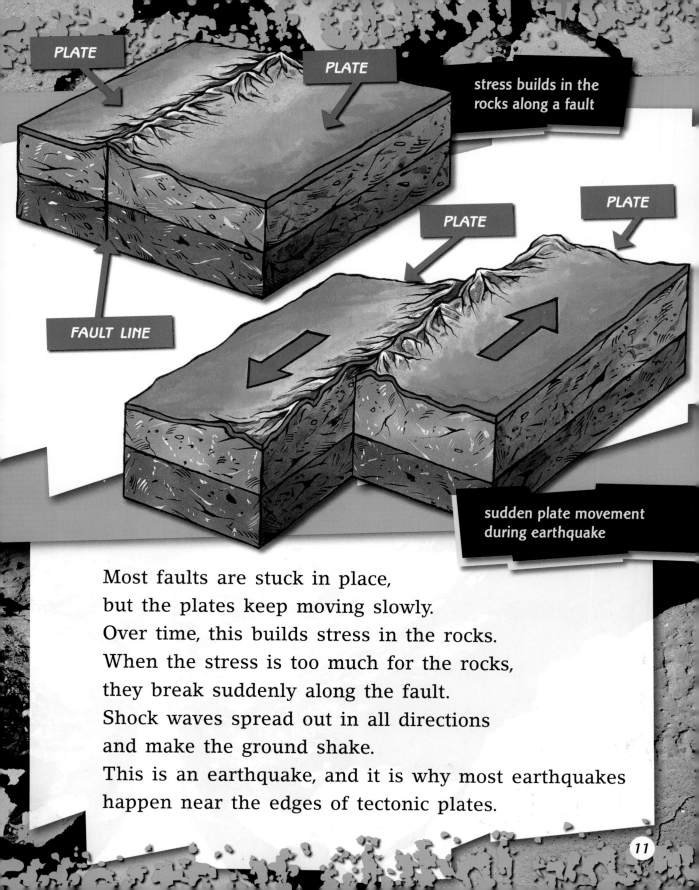

PLATE

PLATE

stress builds in the rocks along a fault

PLATE

PLATE

FAULT LINE

sudden plate movement during earthquake

Most faults are stuck in place,
but the plates keep moving slowly.
Over time, this builds stress in the rocks.
When the stress is too much for the rocks,
they break suddenly along the fault.
Shock waves spread out in all directions
and make the ground shake.
This is an earthquake, and it is why most earthquakes
happen near the edges of tectonic plates.

Chapter 5

MEASURING EARTHQUAKES

Scientists use machines called seismographs
to measure earthquakes.
Information from seismographs helps scientists
to work out the size of an earthquake
and where and when it happened.
A small earthquake makes a small peak
on a seismograph,
and a big earthquake makes a large peak.

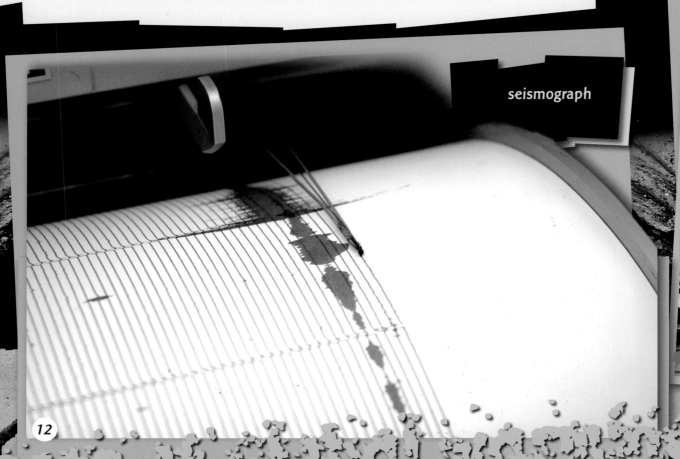

seismograph

Scientists give an earthquake a number on a scale to describe its size.
The higher the number, the bigger the earthquake.
There are several different scales,
but scientists often use the **Magnitude** scale
to measure the size of the earthquake source.
This magnitude 9.5 earthquake in Chile in 1960
was the world's biggest earthquake since 1900.

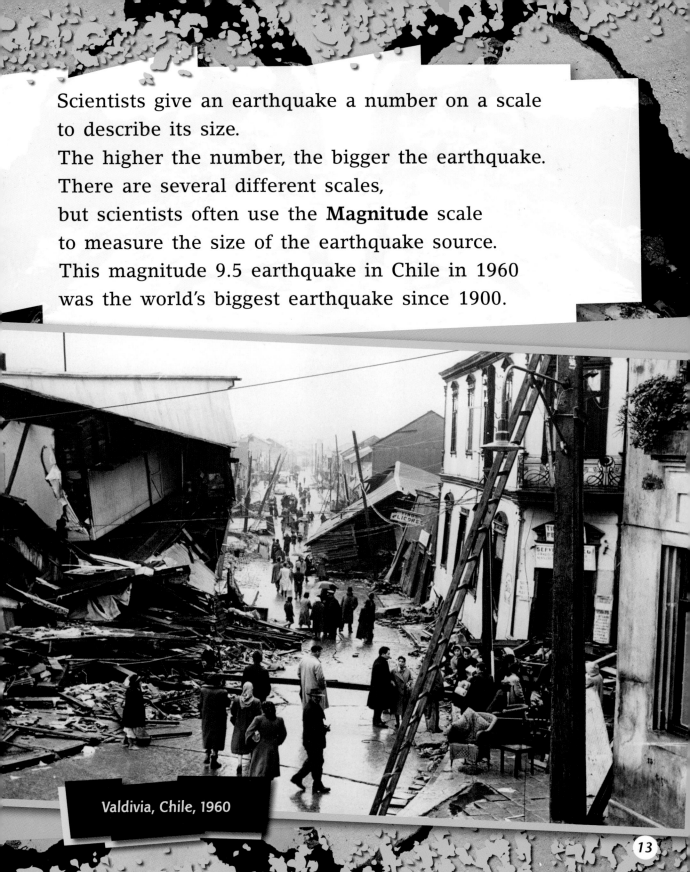

Valdivia, Chile, 1960

The Richter scale measures the largest peak on the recordings made by the seismographs.

The Modified Mercalli scale measures the damage
the earthquake does on the earth's surface.
An earthquake that is high on the Richter scale
may not do a lot of damage in an area where few people live.
The same earthquake would be low
on the Modified Mercalli scale.

Modified Mercalli Scale

Average peak velocity	Intensity value and description	Average peak acceleration
	I. Felt only by a very few people.	
	II. Felt only by a few people at rest, especially on upper floors of buildings.	
	III. Felt by people indoors, especially on upper floors of buildings, but many people do not recognise it as an earthquake. Standing cars may rock slightly. Vibrations similar to the passing of a truck.	
1–2	IV. Felt indoors by many, outdoors by few during the day. At night, some people awakened. Dishes, windows and doors disturbed; walls creak. Sensation like a heavy truck striking a building. Standing cars rock noticeably.	0.015g–0.02g
2–5	V. Felt by nearly everyone; many awakened. Some dishes and windows broken.	0.03g–0.04g
5–8	VI. Felt by all, many frightened. Some heavy furniture moved. Damage slight.	0.06g–0.07g
8–12	VII. Everybody runs outdoors. Not much damage in buildings of good design and construction; lots of damage in poorly built or badly designed structures. Some chimneys broken.	0.10g–0.15g
20–30	VIII. Damage slight in specially designed structures. Lots of damage in many ordinary buildings. Damage great in poorly built structures. Chimneys, monuments and walls fall.	0.25g–0.30g
45–55	IX. Lots of damage in specially designed structures; damage great in many buildings. Cracks in ground.	0.50g–0.55g
more than 60	X. Many structures destroyed. Rails bent.	more than 0.60g
	XI. Few structures remain standing. Bridges destroyed. Large holes in the ground. Rails bent greatly.	
	XII. Damage total. The ground moves in waves. Objects thrown into the air.	

Chapter 6

PREPARING FOR AN EARTHQUAKE

Scientists do not know exactly
when an earthquake will happen,
but they do know that earthquakes are more likely
to happen in some areas.
People living in these areas have to preplan
for an earthquake.

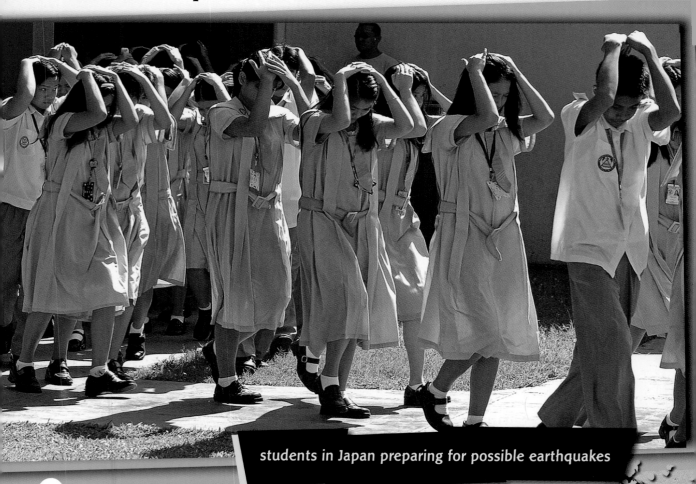

students in Japan preparing for possible earthquakes

Earthquakes are common in Japan.
During an earthquake, school children sit under tables
so that they are protected from falling objects.
If they are outside, they try to move to an open area.
Some people keep a helmet handy in case of
an earthquake.

Chapter 7

EARTHQUAKE SURVIVOR

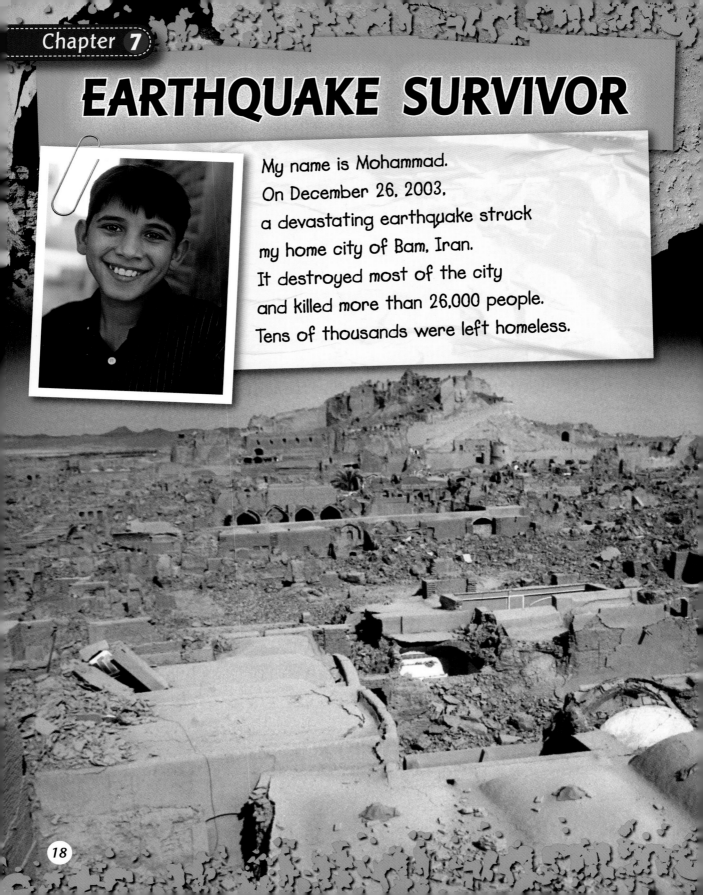

My name is Mohammad.
On December 26, 2003,
a devastating earthquake struck
my home city of Bam, Iran.
It destroyed most of the city
and killed more than 26,000 people.
Tens of thousands were left homeless.

It was early morning when the earthquake struck.
I was asleep with my family outside our home.
A smaller earthquake had woken us earlier in the night,
so we decided to sleep outside.
Our preplanning saved our lives.

When the shake returned,
it seemed like the ground was rising in waves.
I felt so helpless.

Most of the houses were made of mud bricks.
They collapsed, and people were buried beneath them.
All over the city, people helped to dig out survivors.
My father and I helped to rescue some of
our neighbors.

historic Bam, before the earthquake

Bam is over two thousand years old
and was very famous for its history and beauty.
The magnitude 6.6 earthquake turned most of the city
into a pile of dust.

historic Bam, after the earthquake

People from other countries came to help us.
They brought food, water, clothes, tents, and medicine.

People have started to build new homes in Bam, but it will be hard to recover.

Glossary

detectable   able to be felt or detected by scientific instruments

magnitude   the size of something

Index